W9-BGG-558

From Egg
to Butterfly

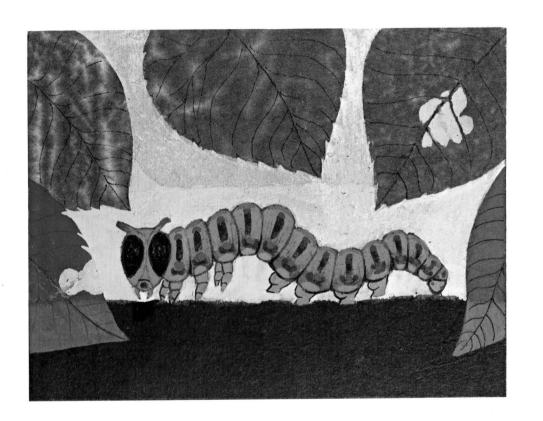

From Egg to Butterfly

Marlene Reidel

 Carolrhoda Books, Inc., Minneapolis

This book is available in two editions:
Library binding by Carolrhoda Books, Inc.
Soft cover by First Avenue Editions
241 First Avenue North
Minneapolis, Minnesota 55401

First published in the United States of America 1981 by
Carolrhoda Books, Inc. All English language rights reserved.

Original edition © 1974 by Sellier Verlag GmbH, Eching bei München,
West Germany, under the title VON DER RAUPE ZUM SCHMETTERLING.
Revised English text © 1981 by Carolrhoda Books, Inc.
Illustrations © 1974 by Sellier Verlag GmbH.

Manufactured in the United States of America.

LIBRARY OF CONGRESS CATALOGING IN PUBLICATION DATA

Reidel, Marlene.
From egg to butterfly.

(A Carolrhoda start to finish book)
Ed. for 1974 published under title: Von der Raupe zum
Schmetterling.
SUMMARY: Describes the metamorphosis of a but-
terfly through its stages of egg, caterpillar, pupa, and
finally butterfly.

1. Butterflies—Metamorphosis—Juvenile literature.
2. Insects—Metamorphosis—Juvenile literature. [1. Butterflies—Metamorphosis.   2. Insects—Metamorphosis]
I. Title.

QL544.2.R44   1981   595.78′9043   81-204
ISBN 0-87614-153-X (lib. bdg.)   AACR1
ISBN 0-87614-458-X (pbk.)

4   5   6   7   8   9   10   97   96   95   94   93   92

From Egg to Butterfly

In the summer beautiful butterflies
seem to be everywhere.
Where did they all come from?

In the spring a mother butterfly finds a leaf
that will be good for her babies to eat.
There she lays her eggs.
The eggs are covered with a sticky substance
so that they will stick to the leaf.
Then the mother flies away.
Her babies will not need her.
They will be able to take care of themselves
from the moment they hatch.

There are over 60,000 different kinds
of butterflies in the world!
Some take only a few days to hatch.
Others take several months.
But none of them hatch as butterflies.
They all hatch as **caterpillars**!
The baby caterpillars are very hungry.
They eat the leaves around them and begin to grow.
Soon they have grown too big for their skins.
Their skins split open, and the caterpillars wriggle out,
complete with new skins.
This happens several times in the life of a caterpillar.

This caterpillar is busy eating leaves and growing.
All the time it has been growing,
its body has been changing inside.
By the fall it is ready to enter the next stage
of its life and become a **pupa** (PYEW-puh).
Most caterpillars that hatch in the spring
are ready for this change in the fall.

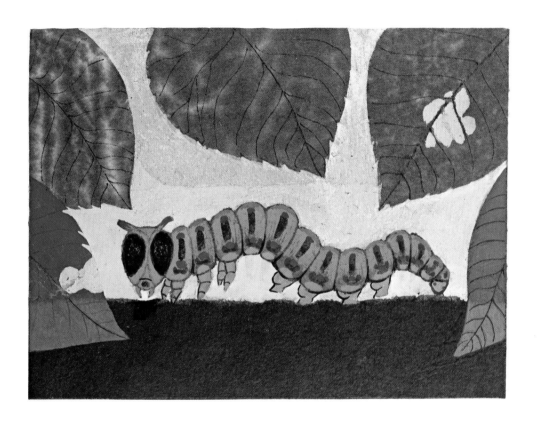

The caterpillar hangs upside down from a piece of bark.
It attaches itself to the bark with a sticky liquid
that comes out of an opening near its mouth.
The caterpillar sheds its skin one last time.
But because the caterpillar's body has been changing,
it no longer looks like a caterpillar underneath.
As the skin peels away, the soft pupa is revealed.
A hard shell called a **chrysalis** (KRIS-uh-lus)
quickly forms around the pupa to protect it.

Protected by the chrysalis,

the pupa hangs from the bark all winter long.

It never moves.

It does not even seem to be alive.

But inside the chrysalis,

a wonderful change is taking place.

The pupa is changing into a butterfly.

By the time spring arrives,
the butterfly's body has grown too big
for the chrysalis.
The chrysalis splits open,
and the butterfly struggles out.
At first its wings are folded and weak.
Its body is soft.
But the butterfly's body soon hardens.
It flaps its wings to make them strong
and then flies away.

The butterfly has now gone through
the four stages of its life.
It has changed from an egg to a caterpillar
to a pupa to a butterfly.
This process of change is called **metamorphosis**
(met-uh-MORE-fuh-sis).
It has taken a whole year to complete.
Metamorphosis is one of nature's most amazing miracles!

**Marlene
Reidel**

MARLENE REIDEL was born in lower Bavaria and was raised on an isolated farm called *Krottenthal.* She is the oldest of seven children.

Ms. Reidel studied ceramics as a girl and then went on to attend the Academy of Fine Arts in Munich. She has written and illustrated many children's books and has received numerous honors and awards for her work, including the German Youth Book Prize, the Most Beautiful German Book of the Year award, the Culture Prize of Eastern Bavaria, and the Special Prize of the German Academy for Children's and Youth Literature.

THE CAROLRHODA

>>> **START**

TO FINISH >>>

BOOKS